Text: Sue Becklake
Consultant: Carole Stott, B.A, FRAS
Illustrations: Sebastian Quigley
Computer illustrations: Mel Pickering
Photo research: Liz Eddison and Laura Cartwright

Art Director: Belinda Webster
Production Director: Lorraine Estelle
Managing Editor: Deborah Kespert
Editor: Samantha Hilton
Designer: Lisa Nutt

U.S. Editorial Team
Associate Editor: Nicole Valaire
Science consultant: Gary Brockman

Jet Propulsion Laboratory: p15; Julian Cotton Photo Library: p45 (right); Mary Evans Picture Library: p27 (right) & p45 (left); NASA: p70; National Maritime Museum Picture Library: p41; Science Photo Library: p51 (top right), p66; SPL/AAO/Royal Observatory Edinburgh: p35 (top); SPL/John Chumack: p37 (top left); SPL/Luke Dodd: p35 (bottom); SPL/Tony Hallas: p43; SPL/ESA/Tom Kinsbergen: p12; SPL/Jerry Lodriguss: p8/9; SPL/Allan Morton/Dennis Milon: p42; SPL/MSSSO, ANU: p31(bottom right); SPL/NASA: p18, p19, p20, p21 (top and bottom), p25, p28, p32 (top right), p49 (top right), p55 (top and bottom), p57, p58, p59, p60, p62, p63, p64 (right), cover; SPL/NASA/Space Telescope Science Institute: p31 (bottom center), p37 (top right), p49 (bottom left and right); SPL/NOAA: p69; SPL/David Nunuk: p32 (bottom); SPL/Arianespace/CNES/David Parker for ESA: p53; SPL/ Pekka Parviainen: p30; SPL/Roger Ressmeyer: p44, p46, p47 (top and bottom), p64 (left), p65, p67; SPL/Royal Observatory Edinburgh: p31 (top right); SPL/US Geological Survey: p27; SPL/John Sandford: p33, p39, cover; Anglo-Australian Observatory: p34; The Stock Market/K. Owaki: p50/51; Tony Stone Images/Marc Chamberlain: p17; Tony Stone Images/Paul Fletcher: p12; Tony Stone Images/Greg Vaughn: p16.

Produced for Scholastic Inc. by Two-Can Publishing Ltd., 346 Old Street, London, EC1V 9NQ, U.K.
Copyright © 1998 by Scholastic Inc. and Two-Can Publishing Ltd.
All rights reserved. Published by Scholastic Inc.

Library of Congress Cataloging-in-Publication Data

Becklake, Sue
All about space / [Sue Becklake]
        p.   cm. — (Scholastic first encyclopedia)
    Includes index
    Summary: Introduces space by explaining such terms as the
universe, solar system, planets, meteors, space stations, and satellites.
    ISBN 0-590-10471-3
    1. Space sciences—Juvenile literature.   [1. Space sciences.
    2. Outer space] I Series.
    QB500.22.A42 1998
    550—dc21   97-12561
                                                        CIP
                                                         AC

12 11 10 9 8 7 6 5 4 3 2 1   9 0/0 01 02

Printed by Wing King Tong in Hong Kong.
Color reproduction by Next Century Ltd., Hong Kong.
First Scholastic printing, February 1999.

All About Space

SCHOLASTIC REFERENCE

New York Toronto London Auckland Sydney

How to use this book

Look it up!
All About Space tells you about the solar system, its planets and moons, astronomy, and space travel. The Contents page at the front of the book lists all of the subjects, or entries, discussed in the book and on which pages they begin.

Cross-references
Above the colored bar on each page there is a list of related entries in this book or any of the other five books in the *Scholastic First Encyclopedia* series, with their book titles. These other entries tell you more about the subject on the page. If there are a lot of related entries, only the book title is given.

Glossary
Words in the book that may be difficult to understand are written in **bold**. The Glossary, which starts on page 72, lists these words in alphabetical order and explains what they mean.

Index
The Index, which starts on page 74, is a list of many of the things mentioned in the book, arranged in alphabetical order, with their page numbers. If you want to read about a subject, look it up in the Index and then turn to the page number given. When a page number is written in *italics*, there will be a picture of the entry on that page.

Contents

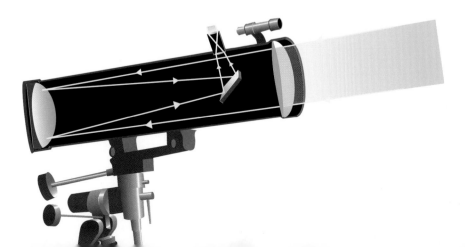

The universe

The universe is the name given to everything that exists. This includes Earth and everything in space, such as the Sun, Moon, and distant stars. The universe is too enormous to imagine. It stretches farther than astronomers can reach with their most powerful telescopes.

Big Bang

Scientists think that, **billions** of years ago, the universe began in a huge explosion, called the Big Bang. Scientists cannot yet explain why this happened. At first, the universe was just **gas**. Then, over billions of years, stars and **planets**, including Earth, slowly began to form from this gas.

▶ The universe is always changing. In space, between the stars, there are huge, glowing clouds of gas and dust called nebulae. Here, new stars begin their lives.

Expanding universe

The universe probably contains billions of galaxies, which are huge groups of stars. These galaxies are all moving away from each other, which means the universe is growing bigger, or expanding. Astronomers do not know if the universe will continue expanding or if it will eventually start to shrink. If it does start to shrink then, billions of years from now, it could squash back together again. Astronomers call this idea the Big Crunch.

Solar system

The **solar system** is the name given to the Sun and everything in space that travels around it. The Sun is the biggest member of the solar system and lies at its center. Nine **planets** are known to travel around it. Earth is one of these planets. Many smaller space objects, including **moons**, asteroids, and comets, are also part of the solar system.

Planets

Mercury, Venus, Earth, and Mars are called **rocky planets** because they are made mostly of rock. Jupiter, Saturn, Uranus, and Neptune are made mostly of **gas** and **liquid**. They are called **gas planets**. Pluto is probably made of rock and ice and is the smallest planet in the solar system.

Orbits

Each planet travels around the Sun following its own invisible path, called an **orbit**. An orbit has an oval shape, called an **ellipse**.

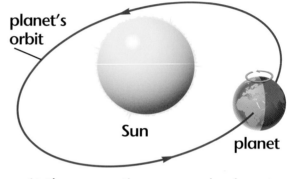

planet's orbit

Sun

planet

At the same time as each planet races along in its orbit, it also spins around.

Pluto

Neptune

Uranus

Moons

A moon is a body of rock that orbits a planet. Some planets, such as Saturn and Jupiter, have large families of moons orbiting them. Earth has only one moon (called the Moon), and Mercury and Venus have none at all. Moons are all different sizes and they are smaller than the planets they orbit.

▼ In the solar system, there are huge distances between the planets. Mercury is the closest to the Sun, and Pluto is the farthest away.

Did you know?

The five planets closest to the Sun are bright enough to be seen in the night sky without a telescope.

Earth travels around the Sun 50 times faster than a supersonic jet.

All the planets are traveling around the Sun in the same direction. They move in the opposite direction to the hands on a clock.

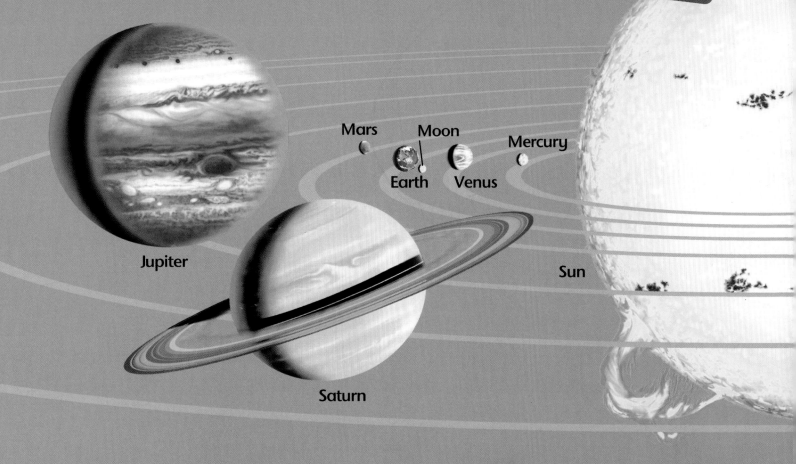

Jupiter

Mars

Moon

Earth

Venus

Mercury

Saturn

Sun

The Sun

The Sun is a medium-sized star. It looks much bigger than the other stars in the sky because it is closer to Earth than they are. Like all stars, the Sun is a huge ball of hot, glowing **gases**. The center of the Sun is so hot that the gases there change in a way that makes **energy**. The Sun sends out this energy as heat and light.

▼ Without the Sun's energy, Earth would be dark, and no plants or animals could live here.

The active Sun
The Sun's surface is always changing. Sometimes, loops of hot, glowing gas, called prominences, hang high above the Sun's surface. Flares, which are giant bursts of energy, rise like bright flames. Often, there are dark patches, called sunspots. These are areas of gas that are cooler than the rest of the Sun.

▼ The Sun's surface bubbles like a giant soup. It is about 60 times hotter than boiling water.

WARNING!
Never look at the Sun, especially not through a telescope or binoculars. You could damage your eyes.

sunspot

prominence

Exploring the Sun

Scientists can learn more about the Sun by sending **spacecraft**, called space probes, into space. In 1990, the *Ulysses* probe left Earth to fly around the Sun's North and South **Poles**.

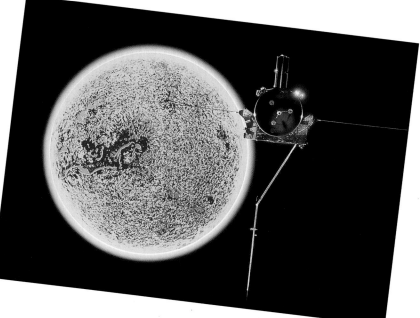

▲ *Ulysses'* journey to the Sun took four years. It collected information and sent it back to scientists on Earth.

Eclipse of the Sun

As the Moon circles around Earth, it sometimes comes directly between the Sun and Earth. The Sun is hidden behind the Moon. The Sun's light is blocked and it goes dark for a short time in some parts of the world. This is called an eclipse.

Sun

Moon

Earth

flare

Mercury

Mercury is the closest **planet** to the Sun. During the day, Mercury is hotter than the hottest desert on Earth, but at night it is freezing cold. This is because there is no **atmosphere** to keep the Sun's heat from escaping. There is no water here, and the surface is covered with **craters**.

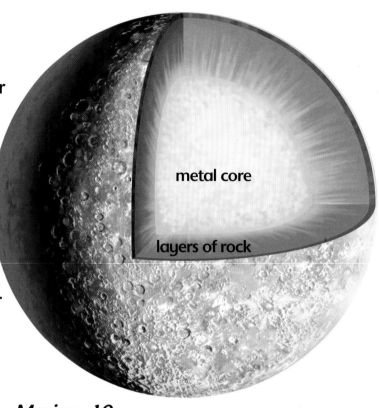

metal core

layers of rock

▶ Mercury is a **rocky planet** with a large metal center, or core, made of iron and nickel.

Spotting Mercury

The planets do not make their own light. They look bright in the night sky only because the Sun is shining on them. Mercury is difficult to see in the sky because it is small and travels close to the bright Sun. Look for it just after sunset or just before sunrise.

Mariner 10

In 1974, the *Mariner 10* space probe visited Mercury. The probe discovered a huge **plain** that is 800 miles across and ringed by high mountains.

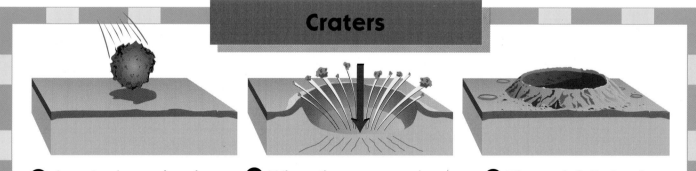

Craters

❶ A crater is made when a rock from space crashes into a planet or **moon** at great speed.

❷ When the space rock lands, it shatters. Broken rock and rock from the surface shoot out in all directions.

❸ The rock falls back to make a ring of hills. A large hollow, or crater, appears on the land.

Venus

Venus is the second **planet** from the Sun and the closest planet to Earth. Like Earth, it is a **rocky planet** and it is almost the same size. But astronauts cannot land on Venus because its clouds trap the Sun's heat, making it even hotter than Mercury.

▶ The surface of Venus is completely hidden by a layer of thick, swirling clouds.

Acid clouds

Space probes that visit Venus have to be made of tough **material** because the planet's clouds contain **acid**. The air on Venus also presses down much harder than the air on Earth, and the first probes that tried to land here were crushed. Later probes lasted just long enough to send a few pictures back to Earth.

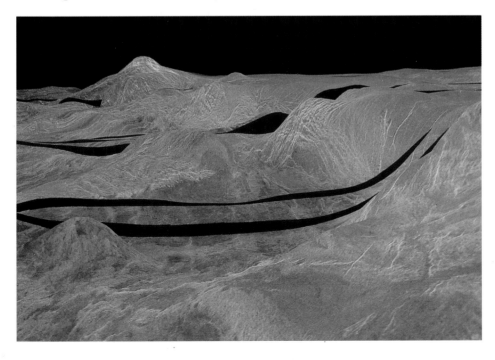

Spotting Venus

Venus can easily be seen from Earth. Except for the Moon, it is the brightest object in the sky. Venus appears just after sunset, when it is called the evening star, and just before sunrise, when it is called the morning star.

◀ In 1990, the *Magellan* space probe visited Venus. Scientists on Earth used information from the space probe to make this picture of Venus's surface.

15

See also Asteroid and meteor, Solar system, The Sun; ANIMALS AND NATURE; OUR PLANET EARTH

Earth

Earth is the third **planet** from the Sun. It is the only planet in the **solar system** known to have life. This is because of Earth's distance from the Sun, which makes it just the right **temperature** for living things to survive. A layer of air surrounds and protects Earth. It contains a **gas** called **oxygen** that humans and other animals must breathe in order to live.

▶ Much of Earth's surface is covered by an ocean of water. From space, the planet looks blue, with white clouds made of droplets of water.

The changing Earth
Millions of years ago, Earth's surface was covered with **craters**. But as time passed, many of these craters wore away. Earth's surface is always changing. Wind and rain wear away the rocks and soil. Water flowing in rivers carries away the soil, carving **valleys** through the land. Ocean waves batter the coastline, forming steep cliffs. **Earthquakes** also change the surface from time to time.

◀ A **volcano** throws out ash and hot melted rock, called lava, from deep inside Earth. The lava cools and hardens, forming rocky layers that build up to form a mountain.

Life on Earth

There are many different kinds of living things on Earth, from huge whales to tiny insects that are too small to see. Animals and plants live in almost every place, from the freezing polar lands, the thickest rain forests, the hottest deserts, to the deepest parts of the ocean.

A year

It takes 365 ¼ days for Earth to travel once around the Sun. This time is called one year. Each planet in the solar system takes a different amount of time to travel around the Sun. So a year is a different length of time for each planet.

▲ This coral reef is teeming with many kinds of fish and plant life. Even the coral itself is living and growing.

Night and day

The Sun is shining on Earth all the time. As Earth spins around, only one side of the planet at a time faces the Sun. This side has daytime. On the other side, where the Sun is not shining, it is nighttime.

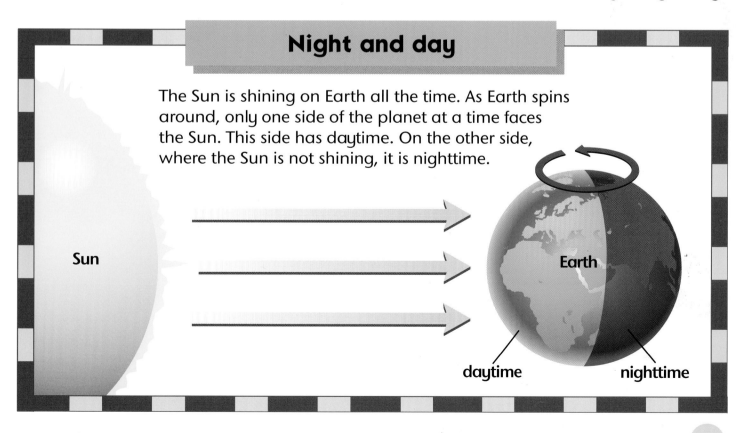

Sun

Earth

daytime   nighttime

The Moon

The Moon is a ball of rock that circles around Earth once every 27 days. The side that faces the Sun is often hotter than boiling water, but the other side is freezing cold. There is no air or water on the Moon, and the surface is dry and dusty. It is the only place in space that astronauts from Earth have visited.

▶ There are dark areas on the Moon. These are really dry land, but long ago, astronomers thought they were filled with water, so they called them seas.

▲ The surface of the Moon is rocky and covered with **craters**. Mountains and hills surround the edges of large, flat **plains**.

Moon shapes

The Moon does not make its own light. It shines in the sky only because the Sun is shining on it all the time. From Earth, the Moon seems to change shape in the sky. This is because it shows a different amount of its sunlit side as it circles around Earth.

new Moon **crescent Moon** **full Moon**

People cannot see a new Moon because the Sun is shining on the side facing away from Earth. A crescent Moon shows only a small part of its sunlit side. A full Moon shows all of its sunlit side.

Exploring the Moon

In 1969, the first astronauts landed on the Moon. This trip was followed by five more missions, the last in 1972. Each time, the astronauts landed on a different part of the Moon. They explored the area near their landing site, set up experiments, and collected Moon rocks to bring back to Earth.

▶ This footprint was made by an astronaut. It will stay on the Moon for thousands of years because there is no wind or rain to blow or wash it away.

Mars

Mars is the farthest **rocky planet** from the Sun. From Earth, it looks reddish in the sky, so Mars is sometimes called the Red Planet. We know of no running water on Mars, but dry riverbeds on its surface show that there probably was water here long ago.

Looking for life on Mars

In 1976, two space probes landed on Mars. They sent back pictures to Earth of a dry, windy desert dotted with **craters** and **canyons**. The *Viking* probes also tested the dust on Mars for signs of life, but they did not find any.

North Pole

Olympus Mons

Valles Marineris

South Pole

▲ Like Earth, Mars has ice at its North and South **Poles**.

▼ The *Viking 2* space probe took this picture of Mars's dusty, rock-covered surface.

Weather on Mars

There are only a few clouds in the Martian sky. These are made of ice, so rain does not fall. Strong winds whip up huge dust storms that sometimes cover the whole **planet**.

Volcanoes and canyons

An enormous canyon, called Valles Marineris, stretches across the middle of Mars. It is ten times longer than the Grand Canyon on Earth. Mars also has several large **volcanoes**, but they are probably all **extinct**.

Missions to Mars

Space probes are now finding out more about Mars. One probe, called *Pathfinder*, has landed on the planet, and others will take pictures of Mars from space. Future missions may bring back some rock to Earth. One day, astronauts may even make the long journey to Mars and back.

▶ Mars has two potato-shaped **moons** called Phobos and Deimos. Deimos is shown here.

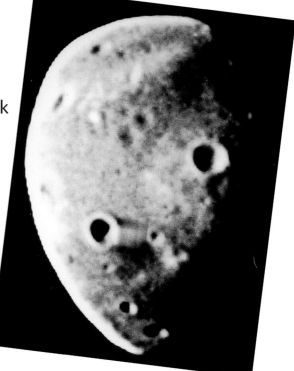

now picture this

Olympus Mons on Mars is the largest volcano in the **solar system**. It is about three times as high as Mount Everest, the highest mountain on Earth.

▲ **Remote control** cars have been built to explore Mars. The first one, called *Sojourner*, crawled up to rocks to find out what substances they contain.

See also Astronomer, Solar system, Space probe

Jupiter

Jupiter is the fifth **planet** from the Sun and the largest planet in the **solar system**. It is often called a **gas** giant because it is bigger than all the other planets put together, and it is made mainly of gas and **liquid**. Jupiter has no solid surface on which a space probe can land.

▶ A thick layer of clouds surrounds Jupiter. The planet's strong winds blow the clouds into orange and white bands.

The Great Red Spot

The Great Red Spot is a huge storm in Jupiter's clouds. It is made of red clouds that swirl around in an oval shape. The Great Red Spot was first noticed over 300 years ago, so this storm has lasted much longer than any storm on Earth.

The Great
Red Spot

▲ The Great Red Spot changes size. At its biggest, it is three times wider than Earth.

Did you know?

Jupiter is more than 11 times wider than Earth. If you placed 11 Earths side by side, they would not quite stretch across the middle of Jupiter.

Jupiter has a thin, faint ring that circles around it. It is made of tiny specks similar to dust.

Jupiter spins around so fast that its middle bulges out.

Jupiter's moons

Jupiter has 16 **moons**—4 large ones and 12 small ones. The large moons are called the Galilean moons. They are named after an astronomer, called Galileo, who discovered them in 1610.

Io is Jupiter's closest moon. It is a blotchy orange-red color and has many **volcanoes**.

Ganymede is the largest moon in the solar system. Its surface is icy and covered with **craters**.

Europa is covered with a smooth layer of ice that **reflects** light from the Sun. There may be an ocean under the ice.

Callisto is covered with craters that are made of ice instead of rock.

Exploring Jupiter

Five space probes have already been to Jupiter. The first four flew past the planet, collecting information to send back to Earth. They gave scientists the first close-up views of Jupiter. The fifth probe, called *Galileo*, went into **orbit** around the planet.

▶ *Pioneer 10,* the first space probe to reach Jupiter, is still in space. It is now speeding far beyond Pluto, which is the farthest planet.

Spotting Jupiter

Jupiter is easy to spot in the night sky. It shines more brightly than any of the stars. The only planet that outshines it is Venus.

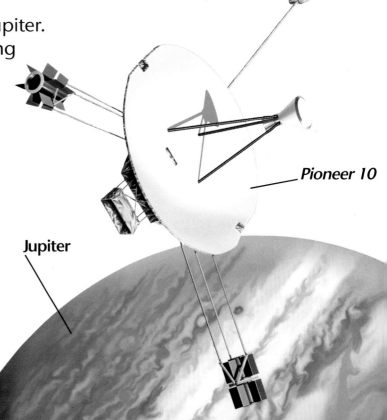

Pioneer 10

Jupiter

Saturn

Saturn is the sixth **planet** from the Sun and the second largest planet in the **solar system**. It is a huge ball made mostly of **gas** and **liquid,** with no solid surface. Thick clouds surround Saturn. Strong winds blow these clouds into bands that stretch around the planet. Saturn has a brilliant set of rings that circle around the middle of the planet.

▲ Like the planet Jupiter, Saturn spins around so fast that it bulges out in the middle.

Saturn's rings

Saturn has a thin but wide system of rings. They are made of millions of icy chunks of rock, each one moving in its own **orbit** around the planet. The icy chunks **reflect** the Sun's light, so the rings shine brightly. Some of these chunks are as fine as dust, while others are the size of a car.

now picture this

Saturn is the lightest planet in the solar system. It would float on water if there were an ocean large enough to hold it.

▲ Colors have been added to this **false color** picture of Saturn's rings to show that they are made of different bands of icy chunks.

Saturn's moons

Saturn has more **moons** than any other planet in the solar system. Astronomers have counted 21 so far, but there may be more. Titan is Saturn's largest moon and the second largest in the solar system. It is covered in thick orange clouds. Under the clouds, there may be a hard icy surface, lakes, or even an enormous ocean.

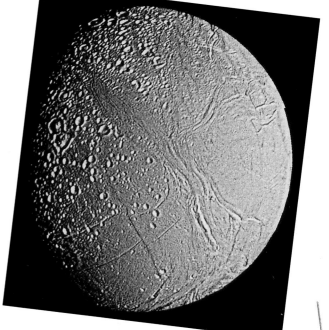

► Most of Saturn's moons are icy. Enceladus has many **craters** as well as smooth areas with long, deep grooves.

Cassini

Cassini is the latest space probe to have been sent to visit Saturn. Unlike earlier probes, *Cassini* will not fly past the planet but will circle around it. Then, it will drop a smaller probe, called *Huygens*, into Titan's clouds to find out what is beneath them.

Saturn

Cassini

► In 2004, after a seven-year journey from Earth, the *Cassini* space probe will arrive at Saturn.

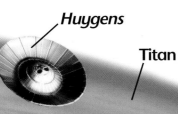

Huygens

Titan

Spotting Saturn

In 1610, an astronomer named Galileo first saw Saturn through a telescope. He was puzzled by its shape, because his telescope was not powerful enough to see that the rings were separate from the planet.

Uranus

Uranus is the seventh **planet** from the Sun. Although it is smaller than the planets Jupiter and Saturn, it is still four times larger than Earth. Uranus is made mostly of **gas** and **liquid**. The planet is surrounded by blue-green clouds that are covered with haze. A few small white clouds can also be seen, blown along by the planet's strong winds.

▶ Uranus is cold because it is so far away from the Sun. Only a little of the Sun's heat can reach this far out into the **solar system**.

Rolling around the Sun

Uranus spins around in a different way than the other planets. Instead of spinning like a top, Uranus "rolls" along, in a way similar to a marble, as it travels around the Sun.

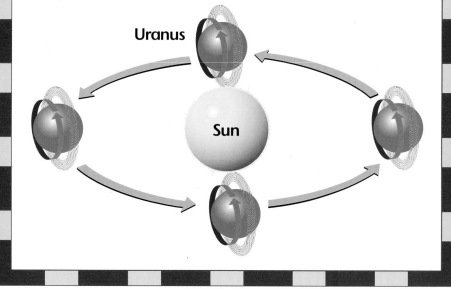

Uranus

Sun

Dark rings
Eleven narrow rings circle around Uranus. The rings do not shine brightly because they are made of chunks of dark **material**. There is also some fine dust among the rings. As the chunks circle around, they bump into one another. This causes them to break up into smaller pieces.

Moons

Uranus has 15 **moons**. The 10 smallest moons are close to the planet and were discovered by the *Voyager 2* space probe. The 5 larger moons are farther away. All the moons and rings "roll" along with Uranus as it travels around the Sun. They seem to be moving up and over the planet, then down again.

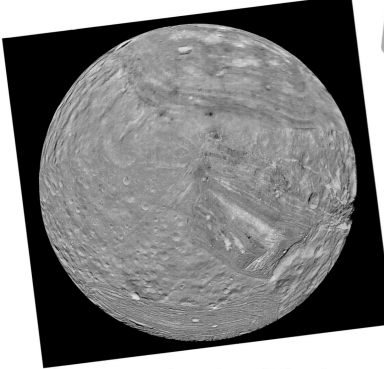

▲ The surface of Miranda, one of Uranus's smallest moons, is covered with tall ridges and cliffs over 12 miles high.

Discovering Uranus

In 1781, an astronomer named William Herschel was using a telescope to study the stars in the night sky. When he first spotted Uranus, he thought it was a comet. Later, he realized he had found a new planet.

Did you know?

Uranus was the first planet to be discovered using a telescope.

As Uranus travels around the Sun, each half of the planet in turn receives sunlight for 42 years, while the other half is in darkness.

Billions of years ago, Uranus may have been hit by something to make it tip over and spin in a different way than all the other planets.

▲ William Herschel accidentally discovered a new planet using a telescope that he built himself.

Neptune

Neptune is the smallest **gas planet** and the farthest gas planet from the Sun. Blue clouds streaked with white clouds cover the surface. Like the **planet** Jupiter, Neptune has a large storm spot. A smaller storm spot sometimes sweeps backward, moving in the opposite direction to the larger one. Hurricane winds blow the spots around the planet.

▶ The Great Dark Spot is a large storm in Neptune's clouds that is as wide as Earth.

Moons and rings

In 1989, the *Voyager 2* space probe flew past Neptune. Astronomers knew that Neptune had two **moons**, but *Voyager 2* discovered that it also has another six moons and a set of four rings.

▲ Triton is Neptune's only large moon and the coldest known place in the **solar system**. The dark streaks may be small **volcanoes**.

The Great Dark Spot

Discovery of Neptune

In the early 1800s, astronomers who had been studying the planet Uranus were puzzled because it was not moving around the Sun exactly as they expected. They thought that there was another planet beyond Uranus.

In the 1840s, two astronomers separately worked out where the new planet should be. In 1846, another astronomer, named Johann Galle, searched in that part of the night sky and found Neptune exactly where the other astronomers had said it would be.

Pluto

Pluto is the smallest **planet** in the **solar system** and the farthest from the Sun. It has never been visited by a space probe, so astronomers know little about it. Pluto is probably made of rock and ice. It has just one known **moon**, called Charon.

Discovering Pluto

After Neptune's discovery, astronomers began searching for another planet. In 1930, an astronomer named Clyde Tombaugh was comparing two pictures of the night sky when he noticed that one of the "stars" had moved. This was Pluto, the planet he had been looking for.

Charon

Pluto

▲ Charon is thought to be about half the size of Pluto. Together, they are sometimes called a double planet.

Pluto's orbit

Pluto takes 248 years to travel once around the Sun. Its **orbit** is slightly tilted, so its path crosses that of Neptune. Neptune and Pluto will not bump into each other because they are always in different parts of their orbits.

Pluto

Neptune

Sun

Probe to Pluto

Pluto is now in the part of its orbit that brings it closest to Earth. So, it is a good time to send a space probe to Pluto and Charon. There is a plan to send two small probes that would travel extremely fast. They would take 10 years to reach Pluto. The mission is called *Pluto Express.*

Comet

A comet is a ball of cosmic snow, ice, and dust that **orbits** the Sun. It is sometimes called a dirty snowball. Comets come from the edges of the **solar system**, beyond the furthest **planet** Pluto. As a comet comes close to the Sun, the Sun's heat turns some of its snow into **gas**, making a glowing cloud in the sky.

▲ In 1997, comet Hale-Bopp appeared in the night sky. It was so bright that you could see it without using a telescope.

A comet's orbit

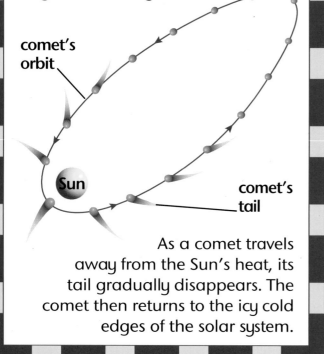

A comet's orbit brings it close to the Sun, then takes it far away again. As a comet nears the Sun, the Sun's **energy** pushes the cloud of gas into a long tail.

comet's orbit

Sun

comet's tail

As a comet travels away from the Sun's heat, its tail gradually disappears. The comet then returns to the icy cold edges of the solar system.

Did you know?

Comets are often named after the person or people who discovered them. Comet Hale-Bopp was spotted by Alan Hale and Thomas Bopp.

The Great Comet of 1843 had a tail that was over 200 million miles long. This is about twice the distance between Earth and the Sun.

The tail of a comet always points away from the Sun.

Halley's comet

Halley's comet is a bright comet that was first seen over 2,000 years ago. It comes near the Sun every 76 years. The comet was named after Edmond Halley, who studied it when it appeared in 1682. He worked out that it would return 76 years later. The comet arrived on time, but Halley was not alive to see it.

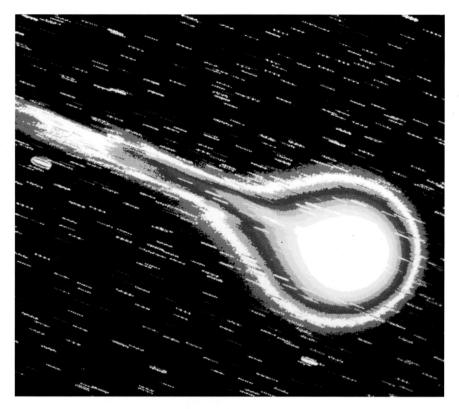

► A comet's icy heart is called a nucleus. The white part of this **false color** photograph shows the nucleus of Halley's comet.

Comet crash

In 1994, astronomers spotted a strange-looking comet. It had broken into pieces that were spread out in a line. Each piece had its own small tail. The pieces were all heading for the planet Jupiter.

One after another, the comet pieces crashed into Jupiter. They hit the planet with such force that they caused huge explosions. Astronomers later found a row of dark scars on Jupiter made by the comet pieces.

▼ As each comet piece hit Jupiter's clouds, the explosion showed up as a bright spot.

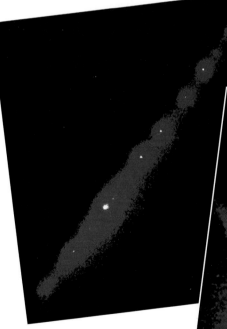

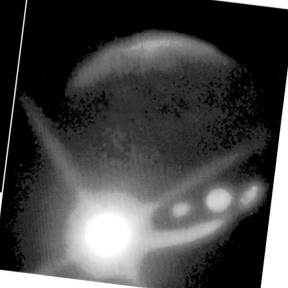

▲ This picture shows the "string of pearls," a line of comet pieces racing toward Jupiter.

Asteroid and meteor

Asteroids are chunks of rock that **orbit** the Sun. They are also called minor **planets**. Most asteroids are found in a band, called the asteroid belt, between the planets Mars and Jupiter. Asteroids are different sizes and most have **irregular** shapes.

Large and small
The largest asteroid is called Ceres and is 600 miles across. Astronomers have spotted thousands of asteroids that are the size of mountains, and there are millions more smaller ones in space.

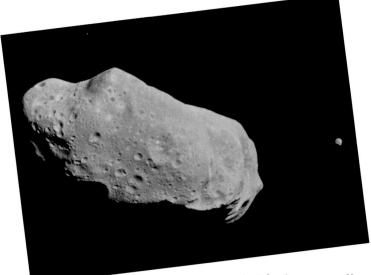

▲ Ida is a small asteroid. It is covered with old **craters** and has one tiny **moon** that circles around it.

Meteor
A meteor is a bright streak of light in the sky. The streak is made when a small piece of space rock enters Earth's **atmosphere**. The rock burns up and the air around it glows red hot.

◄ A meteor is also called a shooting star because it looks like a star falling from the sky.

Meteorite

A meteorite is a large chunk of rock that does not completely burn up when it falls through Earth's atmosphere. It may look like a fireball before hitting the ground. Huge meteorites are rare, but when they hit, they may make a crater on the land.

End of the dinosaurs

Scientists think that, millions of years ago, a huge meteorite crashed into Earth. The explosion caused **billions** of tons of dust to rise up in the air. The dust blocked out the sunlight and it became very cold. Some scientists think that this change in the weather may have killed off all the dinosaurs.

Did you know?

The largest meteorite left on Earth weighs 65 tons, which is about the same weight as 10 large elephants.

In the past, asteroids were probably larger. But over millions of years, they have bumped into one another and broken up into smaller pieces.

NEAR is a space probe that has been sent into space to study one of the asteroids that comes close to Earth.

▼ The meteorite that made this huge crater in Arizona probably weighed about two million tons.

Star

A star is a huge ball of hot, glowing **gases**. It makes **energy** deep within its center. A star shines by sending out this energy into space as heat and light. The closest star to Earth is the Sun. Many stars are even larger than our Sun. They look like tiny points of light in the night sky only because they are so far away.

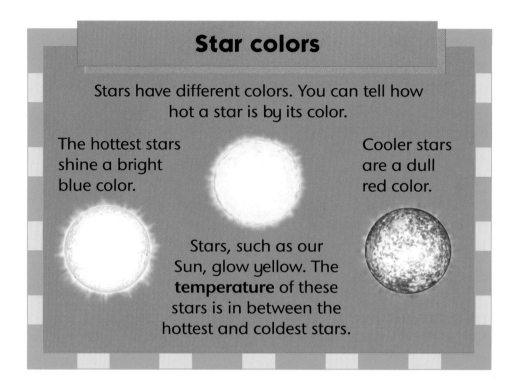

Star colors

Stars have different colors. You can tell how hot a star is by its color.

The hottest stars shine a bright blue color.

Cooler stars are a dull red color.

Stars, such as our Sun, glow yellow. The **temperature** of these stars is in between the hottest and coldest stars.

▲ This group of stars is called the Jewel Box because the red and blue stars shine like colored jewels.

Double stars

Many stars have companions and are called double stars. From Earth, they look like one star. Double stars are so close together that the **gravity** of each star pulls on the other, holding them both in place.

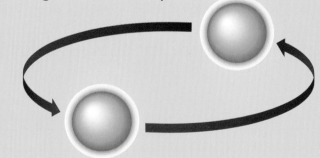

Double stars **orbit** each other. Sometimes, one star passes in front of the other, blocking out some of the other star's light. When this happens, from Earth, the stars look dimmer.

34

Star cluster

A cluster is a group of stars that are all close together. A globular cluster is shaped like a ball. It is a large group of mainly old stars that are packed tightly together. An open cluster contains between ten and a few hundred stars. These stars are much younger and are also farther apart.

▶ The Pleiades is an open cluster of several hundred stars. Only the brightest stars can easily be seen in the sky.

Did you know?

Besides the Sun, Earth's nearest star is Proxima Centauri. It would take thousands of years for a **spacecraft** to travel to this star.

Many globular clusters may be 15 **billion** years old.

Astronomers have just found a star that is so massive, it sends out the same amount of energy in six seconds as the Sun sends out in a whole year.

◀ Omega Centauri is a giant globular cluster that contains about one million stars.

Life of a star

Each star has its own lifetime. It lives for millions or even **billions** of years, but it does not shine forever. The stars in the sky are a mixture of young, middle-aged, and old stars. Massive stars have the shortest lives.

This is because they make a lot of **energy** and use up their supply of **gases** quickly. They live for millions of years. Smaller stars, such as the Sun, make less energy. They continue to shine steadily for billions of years.

Birth of a star

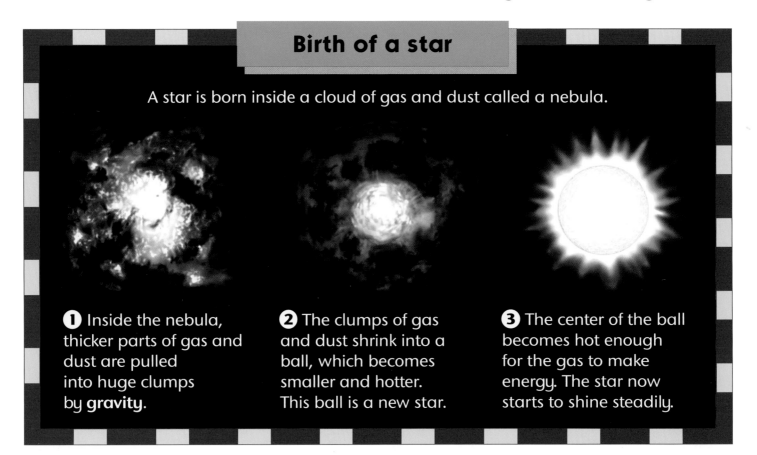

A star is born inside a cloud of gas and dust called a nebula.

1 Inside the nebula, thicker parts of gas and dust are pulled into huge clumps by **gravity**.

2 The clumps of gas and dust shrink into a ball, which becomes smaller and hotter. This ball is a new star.

3 The center of the ball becomes hot enough for the gas to make energy. The star now starts to shine steadily.

Death of a star

Toward the end of its life, an average-sized star, such as the Sun, runs out of energy. The star swells up into a huge, red ball called a red giant. After a few million years, the outer layers of the star puff off into space.

A glowing shell of gas surrounds the remains of the star. The shell is called a planetary nebula. The rest of the star shrinks down to a small, hot star called a white dwarf. The star no longer makes any energy, so over millions of years it gradually fades and dies.

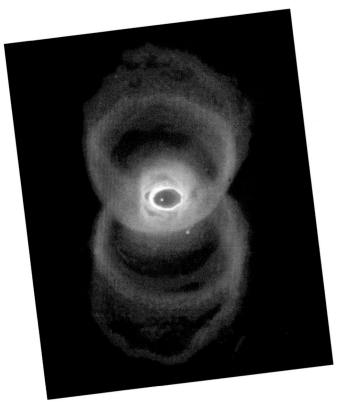

▲ The Orion Nebula is a huge cloud of gas and dust where many new stars are born.

▲ These glowing rings of gas were part of a star that has now died.

Exploding giant
A massive star ends its life in an explosion called a supernova. The star shines brighter than a billion Suns as it blows apart. Then the remains of the star shrink to a hot ball called a neutron star.

Black hole
After a supernova, a massive star may fall in on itself, or collapse, making a **black hole**. Near a black hole, stars are torn apart and gas is sucked in. A black hole's strong gravity even sucks in light.

supernova

black hole

Northern constellations

A constellation is a group of stars that makes a pattern in the sky. This pattern stays the same night after night. As the night passes, the constellations seem to be moving across the sky, but this is only because Earth is spinning around. Astronomers have counted 88 constellations and given each of them a name. People can see different constellations depending on where they live in the world.

▶ These are the main constellations seen in the northern half of the world. This includes countries such as the United States.

Did you know?

The Swan is also known as the Northern Cross because its stars make the shape of a cross.

The Lynx constellation is named after an animal with sharp eyesight, because you need sharp eyesight to spot it.

People use the *North Star* to find their way at night because it shows which direction is north.

Water Carrier

Fishes

Foal

Pegasus

Dolphin

Eagle

Lizard

Swan

Fox

Shield

Cepheus

Lyre

Snake Carrier

Dragon

Little Bear

Hercules

Northern Crown

Hunting Dogs

Snake's Head

Berenice's Hair

Herdsman

Virgin

Twinkling stars

Stars seem to twinkle in the night sky. This happens because people look at the stars through Earth's air, which is always moving. This movement blurs the starlight as it travels to Earth, making the stars twinkle.

Pegasus is named after a magical flying horse in ancient stories.

now picture this

▼ Orion is a large, bright constellation that can be seen from both the northern and southern parts of the world.

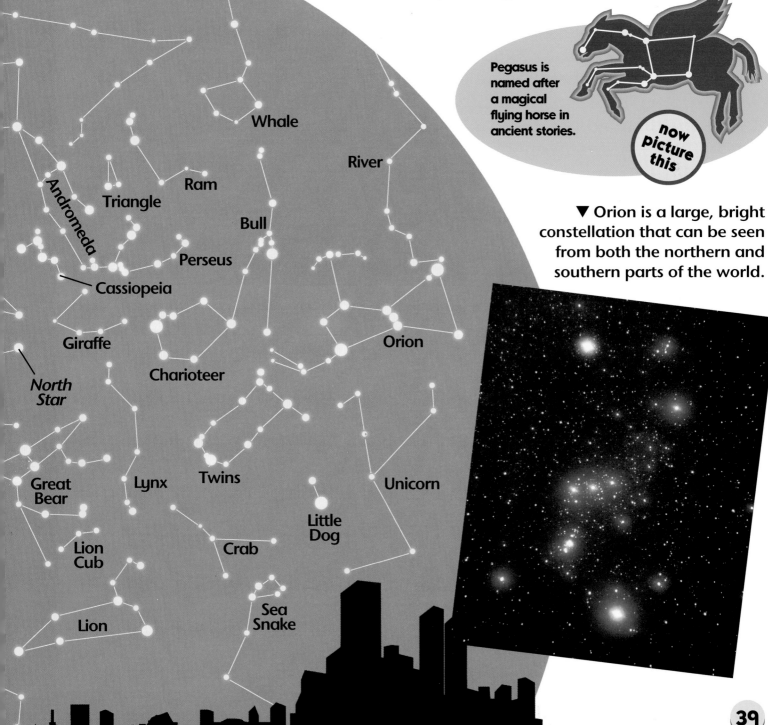

Whale

River

Ram

Triangle

Bull

Perseus

Cassiopeia

Andromeda

Giraffe

Orion

Charioteer

North Star

Great Bear

Lynx

Twins

Unicorn

Little Dog

Lion Cub

Crab

Lion

Sea Snake

See also Northern constellations, Star

Southern constellations

Many constellations, or groups of stars, in the northern half of the world were named 2,000 years ago by the ancient Greeks. But they could not see all of the stars in the southern skies from where they lived. Between the 1500s and 1700s, explorers traveling in the southern half of the world spotted new constellations. They gave them names, such as the Sails and the Stern, after the parts of a ship.

▶ This picture shows the main constellations that people can see from the southern half of the world. This includes countries such as Australia.

Fishes
Whale
River
Sculptor
Phoenix
Furnace
Hare
Swordfish
Net
Orion
Dove
Painter
Great Dog
Sirius
Keel
Stern
Sails
Unicorn
Compass
Little Dog
Air Pump
Sea Snake
Cup

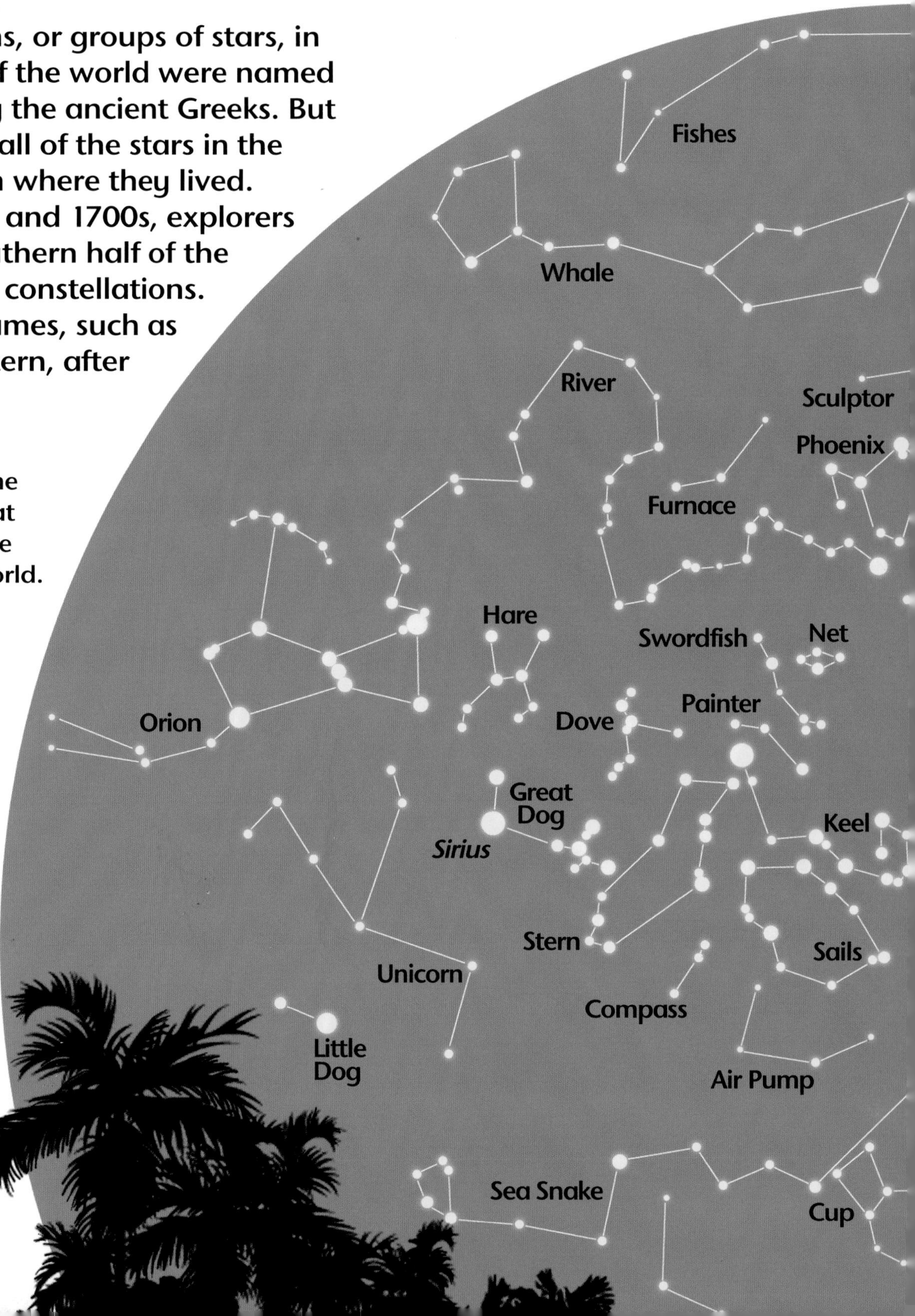

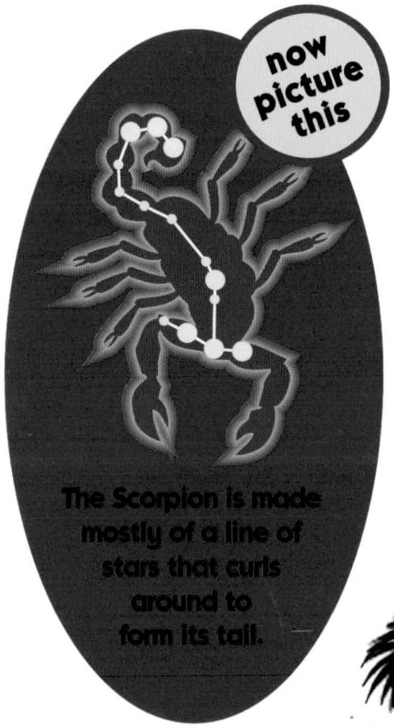

now picture this

The Scorpion is made mostly of a line of stars that curls around to form its tail.

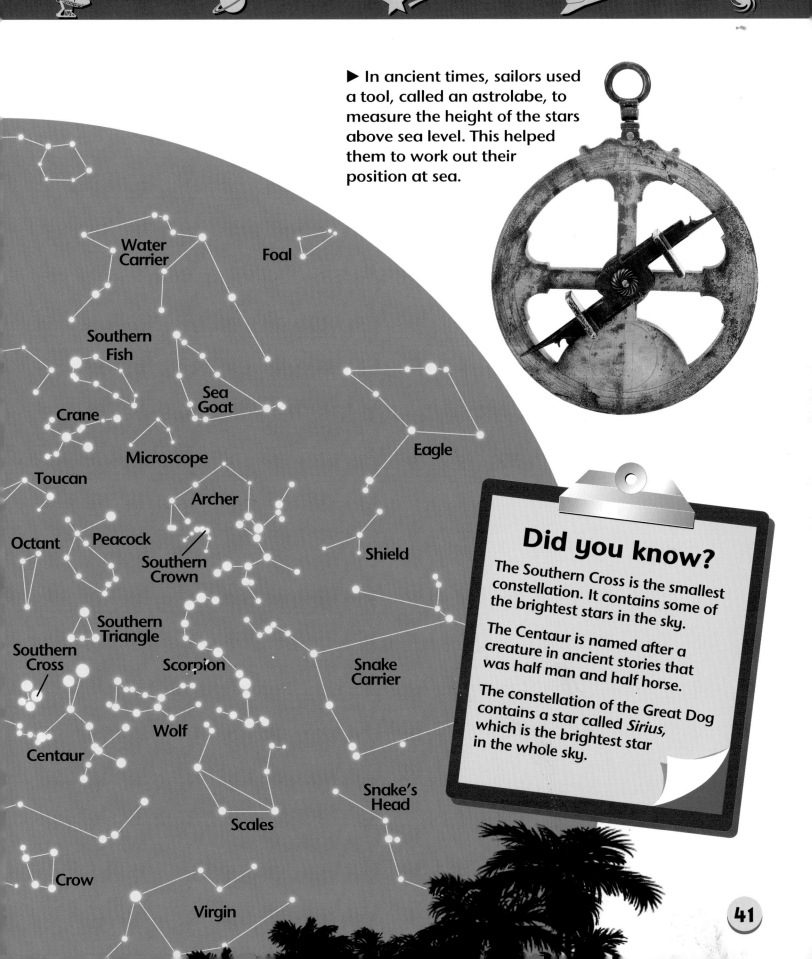

▶ In ancient times, sailors used a tool, called an astrolabe, to measure the height of the stars above sea level. This helped them to work out their position at sea.

Water Carrier

Foal

Southern Fish

Sea Goat

Crane

Microscope

Eagle

Toucan

Archer

Octant

Peacock

Southern Crown

Shield

Southern Triangle

Southern Cross

Scorpion

Snake Carrier

Wolf

Centaur

Snake's Head

Scales

Crow

Virgin

Did you know?

The Southern Cross is the smallest constellation. It contains some of the brightest stars in the sky.

The Centaur is named after a creature in ancient stories that was half man and half horse.

The constellation of the Great Dog contains a star called *Sirius*, which is the brightest star in the whole sky.

See also Astronomer, Astronomy today, Life of a star, Solar system, Star, Telescope, The universe

Galaxy

A galaxy is a huge group of stars, **gas**, dust, and other space objects all held together by **gravity**. Galaxies are different sizes. Even the smallest ones contain millions of stars. In the largest, there are **billions** of stars. Galaxies are scattered throughout space. Astronomers have counted millions of them using powerful telescopes, but they think there are many more still to be found.

Milky Way

The Sun and Earth belong to a galaxy called the Milky Way and lie close to its edge. All the other **planets** in the **solar system,** and the stars that you can see in the sky without a telescope, are part of this galaxy. Astronomers discovered that the Milky Way is shaped like a spiral. You cannot see this whole shape from Earth because you are standing inside the spiral.

▲ On clear, dark nights, part of the Milky Way can be seen from Earth. It looks like a faint, smudged band of light stretching across the sky.

Violent galaxies

Some galaxies shoot out huge high-speed jets of gas far into space. Astronomers think this happens when a **black hole** at the center of the galaxy swallows up some of the stars and gases nearby. There may be a large black hole at the center of most galaxies, including the Milky Way.

Clusters of galaxies

Galaxies are spread unevenly throughout space. They are found together in groups, called clusters. Some clusters contain giant galaxies. These may have grown so large by swallowing up other nearby galaxies.

▲ Andromeda is a nearby galaxy that can be seen without a telescope. It is similar in shape and size to the Milky Way.

Types of galaxies

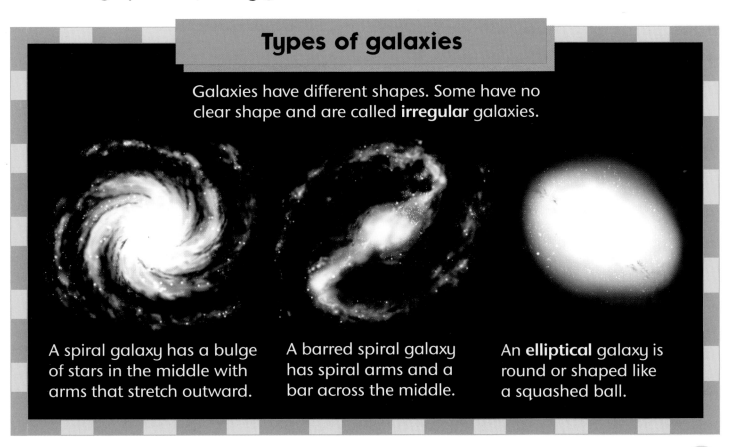

Galaxies have different shapes. Some have no clear shape and are called **irregular** galaxies.

A spiral galaxy has a bulge of stars in the middle with arms that stretch outward.

A barred spiral galaxy has spiral arms and a bar across the middle.

An **elliptical** galaxy is round or shaped like a squashed ball.

Astronomer

An astronomer is someone who studies the Sun, Moon, stars, **planets,** and other objects in space. Many astronomers use powerful telescopes to study these objects. They try to work out the age of the stars and planets, their distances from Earth, what they are made of, and how fast they are traveling.

Ancient astronomy

Long ago, astronomers used the positions of the Sun, Moon, and stars to help people plan their daily lives. By watching the Sun travel across the sky, people could work out the time of day. They also knew when the seasons were changing by studying the positions of the constellations in the sky.

▲ Stonehenge in England is an ancient stone circle. In the past it may have been used as a giant calendar to study the positions of the Sun and Moon throughout the year.

Ideas about the solar system

In 1543, a Polish astronomer named Copernicus said that Earth and all the other planets traveled around the Sun. But people did not believe him. They thought that the Sun and planets traveled around Earth.

▲ Copernicus's ideas changed the way astronomers look at the **solar system**.

In 1610, an Italian astronomer named Galileo noticed that the planet Jupiter had four **moons** circling around it. This showed that everything in the solar system did not travel around Earth. His discovery helped people realize that Copernicus's ideas about the Sun and Earth were correct.

Amateur astronomers

Some astronomers watch the sky as a hobby. They are called amateur astronomers. They use less powerful telescopes than professional astronomers, who mainly study pictures of the sky that have been stored by **computers**. Amateur astronomers spend more time observing the sky. They are often the first people to spot new comets.

▲ On a clear night, amateur astronomers point their telescopes at the sky.

Telescope

A telescope is a special tool that makes stars and **planets** in space look larger and closer. A telescope gathers light and other **energy** from distant objects that are too faint for astronomers to see with just their eyes. A telescope uses this light to make a picture, which astronomers can then study to learn more about space.

▶ Large modern telescopes are protected by a cover, or dome, that opens to show the sky.

How a telescope works

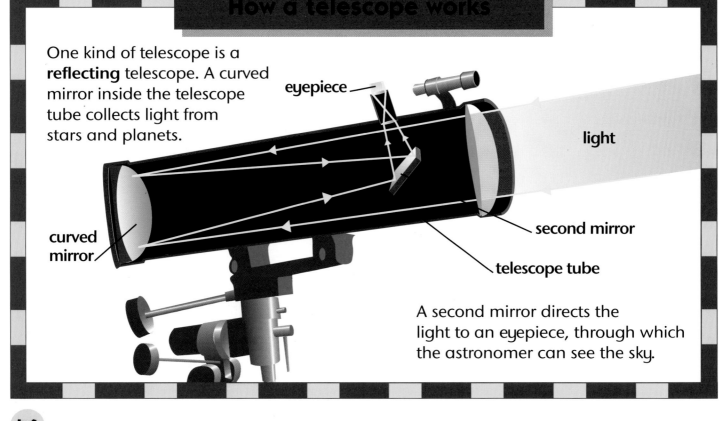

One kind of telescope is a **reflecting** telescope. A curved mirror inside the telescope tube collects light from stars and planets.

eyepiece

light

curved mirror

second mirror

telescope tube

A second mirror directs the light to an eyepiece, through which the astronomer can see the sky.

Observatories

Modern telescopes are usually grouped together at places called observatories. These are often built on the tops of high mountains. Here, the air is clearer and the light from distant stars and galaxies is less blurred than in cities.

Telescope mirrors

A telescope with a large mirror can see farther than one with a small mirror. Some telescopes have many mirrors fitted together. A **computer** makes sure that the mirrors are all pointing in the right direction.

▼ A telescope mirror is made from a curved piece of glass. It must be measured and polished into exactly the right shape.

▲ The Keck Telescope has the world's largest mirror. It is made of 36 smaller mirrors all joined together.

now picture this

The Keck Telescope mirror is 33 feet across. This is the same length as 10 bicycles placed end to end.

Space telescope

A space telescope works in space. It **orbits** Earth above its **atmosphere**. A space telescope works in the same way as a telescope on Earth, but it can see farther and make clearer pictures of objects in space, such as distant stars and galaxies.

On Earth, moving air and dust can blur the pictures taken by telescopes. Out in space, light from distant stars and galaxies travels directly to the space telescope, so its pictures show more detail. A space telescope is controlled by astronomers on Earth.

Hubble Space Telescope

The Hubble Space Telescope is a large telescope that orbits about 360 miles above Earth's surface.

❶ The telescope tube points toward a distant galaxy.

❷ A large mirror collects light from the galaxy.

❸ A smaller mirror **reflects** the light down through a hole in the large mirror. **Instruments** behind the large mirror record a picture of the galaxy.

❹ Radio aerials send the picture as **radio signals** to astronomers on Earth.

❺ **Solar panels** turn sunlight into **electricity** to work the telescope and its instruments.

❻ A cover keeps sunlight from damaging the telescope.

Hubble launch

In 1990, the Hubble Space Telescope was carried into space inside the space shuttle *Discovery*. When the shuttle was at the right distance from Earth, a **remote control** arm lifted the telescope out of the shuttle and sent it into orbit around Earth.

Servicing Hubble

Soon after Hubble was **launched**, astronomers realized that the telescope's mirror was faulty. Its pictures were blurred. In 1993, astronauts visited Hubble in space. They replaced some of the telescope's instruments and added extra mirrors to correct the problem.

▲ This view from inside the shuttle shows the remote control arm releasing Hubble into orbit.

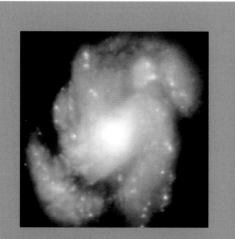

This blurred picture of a spiral galaxy was taken when Hubble had a faulty mirror.

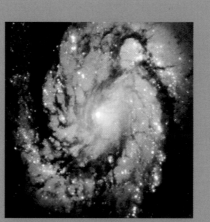

The same galaxy is shown again. This clearer picture was taken after Hubble's mirror had been repaired.

Hubble at work

Hubble has given astronomers close-up pictures of most of the **planets** and **moons** in the **solar system**. It took pictures of a comet as it crashed into the planet Jupiter. It has discovered galaxies that are farther away than any seen by telescopes on Earth. It has looked into clouds of **gas** and dust where new stars are being born.

Astronomy today

Modern astronomers use all kinds of equipment to help them learn about stars and galaxies. They have special telescopes that collect a type of **energy**, called radiation, that they cannot collect with ordinary telescopes. Astronomers use this radiation to make detailed pictures of distant stars and galaxies.

Radio waves

Radio waves are one type of radiation that astronomers collect. Most radio telescopes are huge dishes that collect radio waves from a star or galaxy in the same way that ordinary telescopes gather light. The information from a radio dish is stored on a **computer**, which then makes a picture.

▼ The Very Large Array in New Mexico is a radio telescope made from lots of separate radio dishes that all work together.

Using computers

Today many telescopes work by **remote control,** which means that astronomers do not even have to look through them. A computer directs the telescope to a certain point in the sky and takes photographs of stars and galaxies. A different computer makes the pictures clearer by adding **false colors** to show the hotter or brighter parts of the star or galaxy.

▲ A computer has added bright colors to this picture of a galaxy so that its spiral shape is easier to see.

Modern astronomers

Astronomers use an **instrument** called a spectroscope to look at light from space in more detail. A spectroscope can measure the **temperature** and age of a star. It can also show how far away a galaxy is, what it is made of, and how fast it is traveling. All of these advances have allowed astronomers to build a clearer and more detailed picture of objects in space.

Rocket

A rocket is a **machine** that is powerful enough to carry satellites or astronauts into space. It also sends space probes on missions to other **planets**. A rocket needs to be extremely powerful so that it can reach high speeds and escape the strong pull of Earth's **gravity**.

How a rocket works

Inside a rocket, **fuel** burns incredibly fast, making lots of hot **gas**. The gas rushes out of the nozzles at the back of the rocket, pushing it up into the sky.

fuel tank

oxygen tank

fuel and oxygen burn here

Fuel burns only if it is mixed with **oxygen**. In space, there is no oxygen, so rockets take their own supply with them.

nozzle

hot gas

Rocket stages

Most rockets have two or three parts, called stages. Each stage is similar to a separate rocket and has its own **engine** and fuel. When the rocket takes off, the stages burn up their fuel one at a time and then drop away. This makes the rocket lighter so that it can travel faster. By the time the rocket reaches space, it is speeding along 250 times faster than a car on a highway.

now picture this

During the first three seconds of flight, a rocket burns over half a million gallons of fuel, which is enough to fill an Olympic-sized swimming pool.

Rocket boosters

Rocket boosters are small rockets. They are attached to the main rocket to give it more power at liftoff and extra speed in the air. When their fuel has burned up, they fall away into the ocean.

Launching a rocket

A rocket takes off from a **launch** site. Inside **assembly buildings** and control centers, the rocket is prepared for takeoff. Then a crawler pulls the rocket along a track to the launchpad. From here, the rocket is fired into space.

◄ *Ariane 5* is a rocket that takes large satellites into space. A person can walk faster than the huge crawler that slowly pulls the rocket to the launchpad.

Space mission

A space mission is a journey into space. Astronauts travel into space to visit a space station, carry out experiments, or repair equipment, such as satellites. The farthest astronauts have traveled is to the Moon, but future missions may send astronauts to explore other **planets**, such as Mars.

Missions to the Moon

In July 1969, *Saturn V,* the largest rocket ever built, sent three United States astronauts to the Moon. The mission was called *Apollo 11* and it was followed by six more *Apollo* missions to the Moon.

Did you know?

The *Saturn V* rocket, which took the first astronauts to the Moon, was as tall as a 36-story building

No one has been to the Moon since the last *Apollo* mission in 1972.

Inside the *Apollo* command module, where the astronauts lived for one week, there was as much room as there is inside a family car.

Apollo spacecraft

This part of *Saturn V,* called the *Apollo* **spacecraft,** carried the astronauts to the Moon after they had blasted out of Earth's **orbit.**

The service module supplied the astronauts with **oxygen, electricity,** and water.

The *Apollo* command module is where the astronauts lived.

The lunar lander took the astronauts down to the Moon's surface.

Journey to the Moon

The first *Apollo* mission to the Moon took three days. When the three astronauts arrived, one astronaut stayed in the *Apollo* spacecraft, which orbited the Moon. The other two astronauts flew down to the Moon inside the lunar lander. After nearly one day exploring the Moon's surface, the astronauts flew back up to the *Apollo* spacecraft and returned to Earth.

▶ This astronaut is beside the United States flag, which seems to be blowing in the wind. Actually, the flag is held up with wire because there is no wind on the Moon to blow it.

▲ During the last three missions, *Apollo* astronauts took a car with them, called a lunar rover, so that they could explore more of the Moon's surface.

Moon visits

The *Apollo* astronauts carried out experiments to record shaking movements on the Moon's surface, called **moonquakes**. They also drilled 10 feet below the surface to take samples of rock to bring back to Earth. The *Apollo* missions brought back a total of about 840 pounds of rock, which weighs almost the same as 15 six-year-old children. All of these experiments helped scientists on Earth figure out the age of the Moon and told them what kinds of rock lie beneath its surface.

Mission control

A space mission is controlled by people on Earth. There are usually two control centers. **Launch** control is at the launch site. Here, the **spacecraft** is fitted together, filled with **fuel**, then fired into space. When the spacecraft is safely in space, people at mission control take over. They keep in touch with the astronauts on board the spacecraft.

Keeping in touch

At mission control, teams of people look after each part of the mission. They check that the spacecraft is heading in the right direction and that there is plenty of **oxygen** and fuel. People at mission control stay in touch with the astronauts day and night. They even play music to the astronauts to wake them up in the morning.

Space rescue

In 1970, there was an emergency in space. Three *Apollo 13* astronauts were traveling to the Moon when an explosion blew a large hole in part of their spacecraft. Back on Earth, mission control helped the astronauts find a way home. The astronauts began to run out of oxygen, so they crawled into the undamaged part of their spacecraft, where they lived until they safely reached Earth.

▲ During a mission, huge **computer** screens flash information about the spacecraft and live pictures of the astronauts.

▲ The *Apollo 13* spacecraft landed in the ocean, where a rescue ship was waiting to pick up the astronauts.

Space shuttle

A space shuttle is a **spacecraft** that can fly into space and back to Earth many times. It can take astronauts to a space station, or **launch** space probes and satellites. A shuttle has several parts. The shuttle orbiter carries the astronauts into space. The other parts are a large **fuel** tank and two booster rockets.

▶ The space shuttle *Columbia* is covered with thousands of special tiles that keep it from burning up as it reenters Earth's **atmosphere**.

Takeoff and flight

On the launchpad, the space shuttle takes off like a rocket.

❶ The boosters and fuel tank add their power to the shuttle's own **engines** to help it take off.

❷ The boosters use up their fuel, drop away from the shuttle, and land in the ocean. They can be used again.

❸ The fuel tank uses up its fuel and falls away. This is the only part of the shuttle that cannot be reused.

❹ In space, the shuttle orbiter uses its smaller rocket engines to move. It **orbits** Earth until its mission is over.

Inside the shuttle

Most shuttle missions last for about 9 or 10 days. Inside the shuttle orbiter, there is room for about seven astronauts. On some flights, an extra room, called Spacelab, is added to the shuttle.

Equipment, such as experiments, is stored inside the payload bay.

Inside the flight deck are the controls for the shuttle pilot.

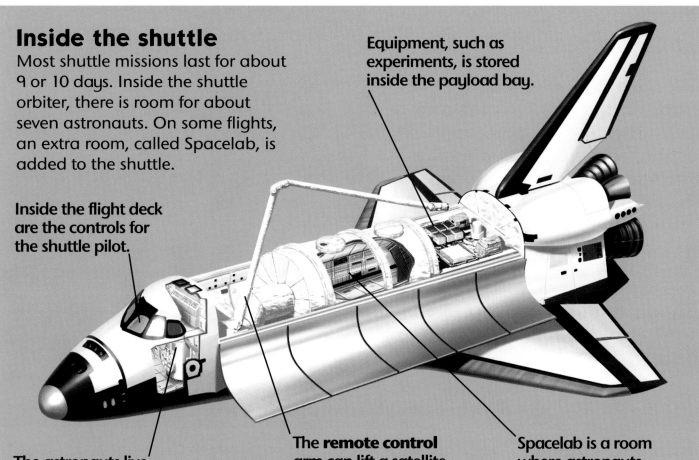

The astronauts live and work in this cabin.

The **remote control** arm can lift a satellite and put it into orbit.

Spacelab is a room where astronauts can do experiments.

Return to Earth

After each mission, a shuttle slows down its engines and **gravity** pulls it to Earth at great speed. The shuttle is traveling so fast that it becomes extremely hot. The pilot then switches off the engines and the shuttle lands on a long runway.

▶ A shuttle lands so fast that it needs a parachute to help slow it down.

Space station

A space station is a home in space that **orbits** Earth. Astronauts live here and carry out experiments to learn more about how space affects people. In a space station, there is plenty of food and water, and enough air for astronauts to breathe.

Mir

In 1986, Russia **launched** the *Mir* space station. Several cosmonauts, which is the Russian name for astronauts, live here for months at a time. Each month, **spacecraft** travel up from Earth, bringing food, water, and equipment.

Building a space station

A space station is built in small parts. These small parts, called modules, are sent into space, one at a time, by a rocket. In space, astronauts fit the modules together to make a large space station. *International Space Station* is the latest space station to be built. It will be launched into space over the next five years.

◀ In 1995, the **crew** of the space shuttle *Atlantis* joined the crew on board the *Mir* space station, making a record total of 10 people inside one spacecraft.

▼ *International Space Station* is a new space station being built by many different countries.

Large **solar panels** turn sunlight into **electricity** to power the space station.

Radio aerials send **radio signals** to keep the astronauts in touch with Earth and other spacecraft.

The controls and **fuel** that work the space station are stored here.

A **remote control** arm holds and moves equipment around.

The astronauts work inside this module.

The astronauts live inside this module.

In an emergency, the astronauts can use this spacecraft to return to Earth.

Early space stations

In 1971, Russia launched the first space station. It was called *Salyut,* and three cosmonauts spent 23 days on board. They discovered what it was like to live and work in space. In 1973, the United States launched *Skylab.* The astronauts who lived on board took thousands of pictures of the Sun and Earth and carried out many experiments. In 1979, *Skylab* fell to Earth and broke apart. Most of the parts fell into the ocean, but some parts fell on Australia.

Astronaut

An astronaut is a person who travels into space to carry out experiments and repairs and to explore new places. The word astronaut means "star traveler," but the farthest any astronaut has been is to the Moon. To survive in space, an astronaut stays in a **spacecraft** or wears a space suit.

How to become an astronaut

Each year, thousands of people apply to go to astronaut training school, but only a few are chosen. To be an astronaut, you must be fit and healthy and have studied science. If you want to fly a spacecraft, you need to have lots of experience flying airplanes.

Space suit

A space suit keeps an astronaut alive outside the spacecraft. It holds air to breathe and keeps the astronaut's body from becoming too hot or too cold.

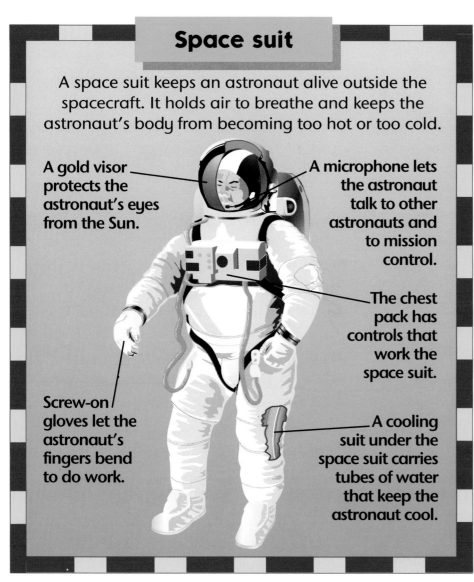

A gold visor protects the astronaut's eyes from the Sun.

A microphone lets the astronaut talk to other astronauts and to mission control.

The chest pack has controls that work the space suit.

Screw-on gloves let the astronaut's fingers bend to do work.

A cooling suit under the space suit carries tubes of water that keep the astronaut cool.

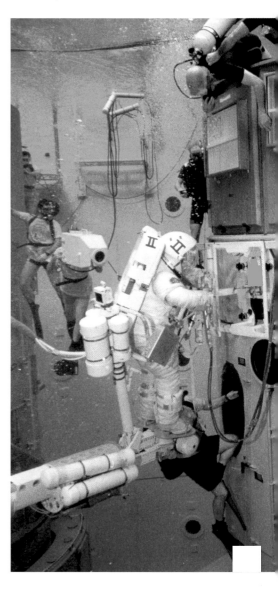

Training

Before astronauts travel into space, they spend months training and practicing everything they will do when they arrive. Space shuttle pilots learn to fly a model of the shuttle. The rest of the **crew** practices everyday things such as cooking and bathing.

▶ During a spacewalk, astronauts work outside their spacecraft, making repairs or testing new tools and equipment.

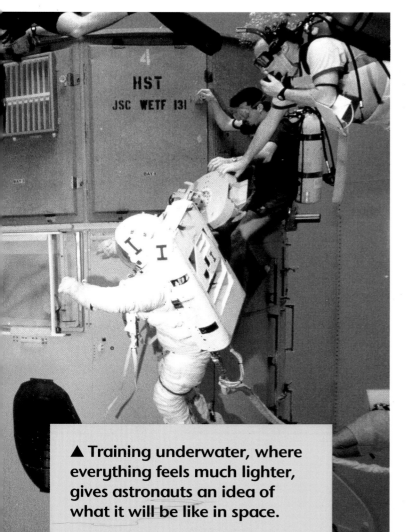

▲ Training underwater, where everything feels much lighter, gives astronauts an idea of what it will be like in space.

Manned Maneuvering Unit

Some astronauts wear a **machine**, called a Manned Maneuvering Unit or MMU for short, to move around easily in space. An MMU has **gas** jets, called thrusters, that fire to move the astronaut in any direction.

▲ An MMU is like a flying armchair. It has flight controls on the ends of the armrests, which the astronaut can work with his hands.

Life in a spacecraft

In a **spacecraft**, people and things do not seem to have any weight. This is called **weightlessness**. If you let go of an object in a spacecraft, it will not fall to the floor as it does on Earth. Instead, it will float away. Astronauts float around in the spacecraft, too. To stay still, they push their feet into special loops attached to the spacecraft.

▲ In a spacecraft there is no up or down, so astronauts can float along the walls and ceiling.

Eating in space

Astronauts eat the same kinds of food on board a spacecraft as they do on Earth. Some food is dried to make it lighter, and hot or cold water is added to it at mealtimes. Astronauts drink through straws to keep **liquids** from floating away.

Sleeping in space

Astronauts sleep in special space beds. The space beds are fixed to a wall, so the astronauts look as though they are sleeping standing up. It is noisy inside a spacecraft, so the astronauts may wear earplugs to help them sleep. As the spacecraft flies past the Sun, sunlight floods in through the windows. Some astronauts wear eye masks to block out the light.

▼ This astronaut is testing a bed that may be used on a future space station.

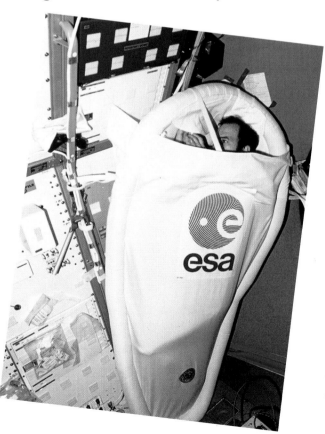

Did you know?

In space, weightlessness makes astronauts grow about one inch, but they go back to their normal heights when they return to Earth.

When an astronaut has a haircut in space, the clippings are sucked up by a special vacuum cleaner.

Some astronauts suffer from space sickness, which is similar to car sickness on Earth.

Keeping fit

In space, where our bodies are weightless, our muscles do not have to work hard, so they become weak. To keep fit, astronauts strap themselves to a rowing or cycling **machine** and exercise every day.

Staying clean

In a spacecraft, everything has to be kept very clean, because germs can spread quickly. A space shuttle has a toilet that sucks away waste with a flow of air. Astronauts use wet and dry towels to keep clean and fresh.

▼ Future space stations may have a shower stall similar to this one. A tube sucks up water droplets when the astronaut finishes washing herself.

Space probe

A space probe is a **machine** sent from Earth by a rocket or space shuttle to explore space. Probes do not carry astronauts on board and they usually do not return to Earth. When a probe arrives at a **planet** or **moon**, it sends back pictures and information to Earth. Some probes fly past a planet, while others **orbit** it or land on the surface for a closer look.

Viking

In 1976, two probes called *Viking 1* and *2* reached the planet Mars. Each probe had two parts. One part orbited Mars, while the other part, called the lander, traveled to the surface. Both landers had scoops to take soil samples and equipment to test them. They also measured the strength of the winds and the **temperature** of the air.

▲ The landers carried by the *Viking* space probes were fitted with cameras. They took over 4,500 pictures of Mars's surface.

Voyager

In 1977, two space probes, called *Voyager 1* and *2*, started on their incredible journeys to the distant **gas planets**. First they flew to Jupiter, then on to Saturn to study the rings around this planet in detail. After this, *Voyager 2* continued on to Uranus and Neptune and sent back close-up pictures of the planets' cloudy surfaces. Both probes are now heading to the outer edges of the **solar system**.

Galileo

In 1995, the *Galileo* space probe arrived at the planet Jupiter. It dropped a smaller probe by parachute into Jupiter's thick clouds. This smaller probe sent information about the layers of clouds up to the main probe, which in turn sent the information to scientists on Earth.

▲ *Galileo* is still watching Jupiter. Its orbit also takes it close to the planet's four largest moons, where it can take pictures of their surfaces.

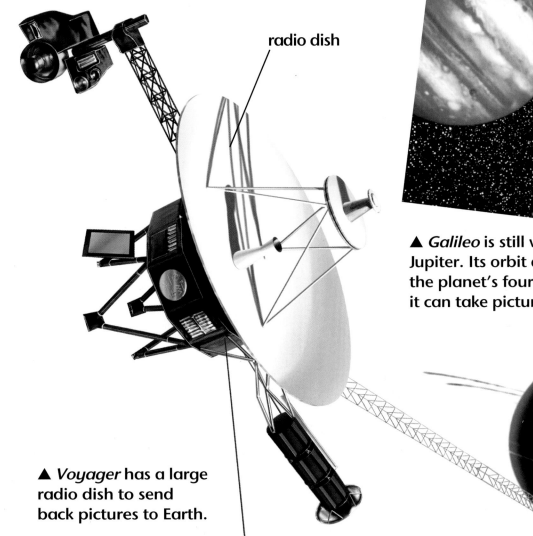

radio dish

Neptune

▲ *Voyager* has a large radio dish to send back pictures to Earth.

Satellite

A satellite is a **machine** that **orbits** Earth. There are many kinds of satellites. Some gather information about Earth's weather, while others send messages instantly from one part of the world to another. Satellites have **radio aerials** to keep in touch with people on Earth. **Solar panels** turn the Sun's light into **electricity** and keep the satellite working.

Launching a satellite

Powerful rockets carry most satellites into space. The satellite is protected by a cover until the rocket reaches space.

rocket

satellite

cover

In space, the cover is thrown off. The rocket boosts the satellite into orbit around Earth.

Communications satellite

A communications satellite sends television programs and telephone calls from one part of the world to another.

Weather satellite

A weather satellite watches the clouds and measures the strength of the winds. It can also record the **temperature** of the land, sea, and air. This information is sent down to weather stations on Earth.

Navigation satellite

A navigation satellite sends out **radio signals** to people such as sailors, soldiers, and airline pilots. The signals help them to navigate, or find their way.

Earth-watching satellite

Some satellites look down on Earth and spot **pollution** in the air and in the ocean, or smoke from forest fires. They also help track wild animals, such as polar bears, to see how far they roam looking for food.

▲ Satellite pictures can warn scientists when a fierce storm, such as a hurricane, is coming.

Space science

Space scientists design rockets and space probes to explore space. They also develop new kinds of equipment to make life in space safer and more comfortable for astronauts. Many of these scientific discoveries are useful to people in their daily lives.

Experiments in space

In space, astronauts carry out all kinds of experiments. The **weightlessness** of space helps them make special drugs used in medicines for people on Earth. Astronauts also carry out medical tests on one another to find out what happens to their bodies in space.

▲ Astronauts wear special equipment to test how weightlessness affects their muscles and bones.

Checkups in space

In space, astronauts stick special pads, called sensors, on their bodies. The pads measure each astronaut's **temperature** and heartbeat. This information is sent down to Earth so that doctors can make sure the astronauts are healthy. Today similar equipment is used in hospitals to check the health of patients.

Did you know?

In 1973, two spiders called Anita and Arabella were taken to live on board the *Skylab* space station. They proved that spiders could spin webs in space as well as on Earth.

Plants have been grown in space to see if they are affected by weightlessness. They grew normally, but some of the plants' roots grew up instead of down.

Keeping in touch

Developments in space help people communicate with one another on Earth. Satellites above Earth's surface can send live pictures of an event, such as the Olympic games, all around the world. People also use small, powerful **computers** similar to those designed by space scientists for use on board **spacecraft**.

The future of space

Scientists are always trying to find out more about space. In the future, there might be large space cities where people could live. Food might be grown in special areas, and there might be factories and schools.

now picture this

In the future, it might even be possible to take a vacation in space.

Space spin-offs

A space spin-off is something that was made for life in space, but is now also used by people on Earth.

A foil blanket kept the *Apollo* spacecraft from becoming too hot or too cold. Marathon runners wear foil blankets to keep themselves warm after a race.

Velcro is a tape used in space to keep things from floating around. On Earth, it is used to fasten shoes, clothes, and bags.

In space, nonstick coatings are used to make parts of a **machine** move smoothly. These are similar to the coatings inside some saucepans.

In space, food is freeze-dried to keep it light and fresh. On Earth, instant coffee is also kept fresh in this way.

Glossary

Acid A powerful substance that can eat into metal and damage a person's skin.

Assembly building A large building where **machines**, such as **spacecraft**, are put together and tested.

Atmosphere A layer of **gas** that surrounds a **planet, moon,** or star. Earth's atmosphere, called the air, is a mixture of different gases.

Billion A number meaning one thousand million, written as 1,000,000,000.

Black hole The remains of a giant star that has exploded. Its **gravity** is so strong that it sucks in everything around it, even light.

Canyon A deep, rocky passage with steep sides that lies between mountains or hills.

Computer A **machine** that works like an electronic brain. It stores lots of information and is used to control other machines, such as telescopes and **spacecraft**.

Crater A round, shallow hole in the ground, which is made when a rock from space hits a **planet** or **moon**.

Crew The people who live and work on a space station or a **spacecraft**, such as a space shuttle.

Earthquake A violent shaking of the ground that happens when Earth's surface moves suddenly.

Electricity A kind of **energy** that makes **spacecraft**, satellites, or even washing machines work.

Ellipse A shape that is almost round like a circle or long and thin like a squashed oval.

Energy The force that makes things move or work. Energy can also be seen as light or felt as heat.

Engine The part of a **machine**, such as a rocket or a **spacecraft**, that makes it move.

Extinct No longer living or active. A **volcano** that has not thrown out any hot ash or melted rock for a long time is called extinct.

False color When scientists add bright colors to a photograph of an object in space, such as a galaxy, to make it look much clearer.

Fuel **Material** that burns inside an **engine** and makes it work.

Gas A substance, such as air, that has no shape and can only be felt when it moves.

Gas planet A **planet** that circles the Sun or another star and is made mainly of **gases** and **liquids**, with no solid surface for a **spacecraft** to land on.

Gravity A force pulling two objects together. Earth's gravity pulls everything near it down to the ground.

Instrument Something that is built to do a special job. A telescope is an instrument for studying stars and **planets**.

Irregular Something that has an uneven shape.

Launch To lift off from Earth on a journey into space.

Liquid A runny substance with no fixed shape, such as water flowing in a river.

Machine Something that moves or does useful work, such as a **spacecraft**.

Material The substance that an object is made of.

Moon An object in space that travels around a larger object, such as a **planet**.

Moonquakes A shaking movement on the Moon's surface, which is similar to an **earthquake** on Earth.

Orbit The curved path of an object as it travels in space around a larger object.

Oxygen A **gas** in the air that animals need to breathe to stay alive.

Plain A flat area of land without any high mountains or deep **valleys**.

Planet A large, round object in space that travels around the Sun or another star.

Poles The farthest points of north and south on a **planet** or **moon**.

Pollution Unwanted **material** that spills into the air, sea, or land, and damages it.

Radio aerial An **instrument** that sends out or picks up messages from satellites and probes.

Radio signals Invisible rays that travel through space carrying information that can be changed into sounds or pictures.

Reflect To bounce off something. A mirror reflects light, which means that light bounces off the mirror, letting you see your reflection.

Remote control Sending messages to something far away to tell it what to do.

Rocky planet A **planet** that travels around the Sun or another star and is made of rock with a hard outer surface.

Solar panel Large panels on a satellite or **spacecraft** that turn the Sun's light into **electricity**.

Solar system All of the **planets, moons,** comets, and rocks that travel around the Sun.

Spacecraft A vehicle that flies in space. It may carry astronauts or it may be controlled by people on Earth.

Temperature How hot or cold something is.

Valleys Low land lying between mountains and hills.

Volcano An opening on Earth's surface where ash and hot melted rock explode out from deep beneath the surface.

Weightlessness Floating in space and feeling as if you weigh nothing.

Index

T

U

V

W

Y